The
WILLIAM SCHAFF

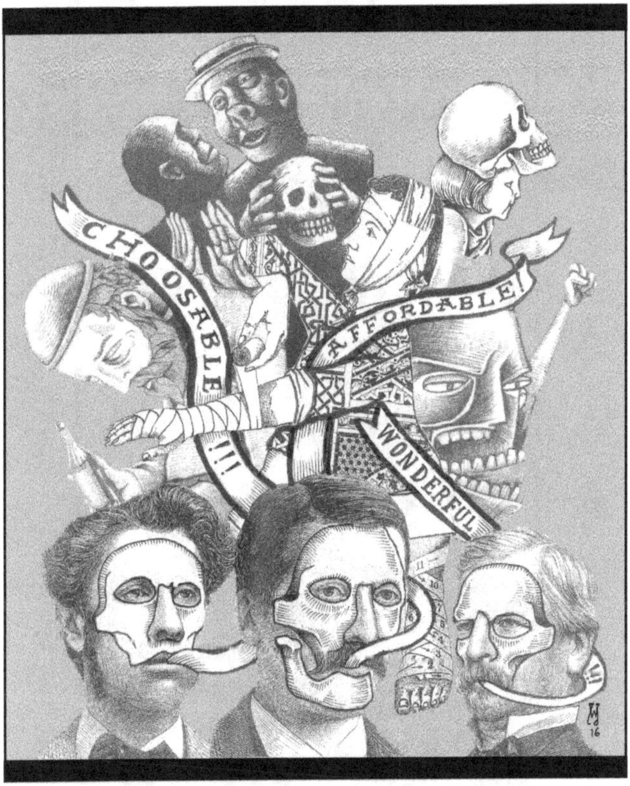

Gallery
of
ART

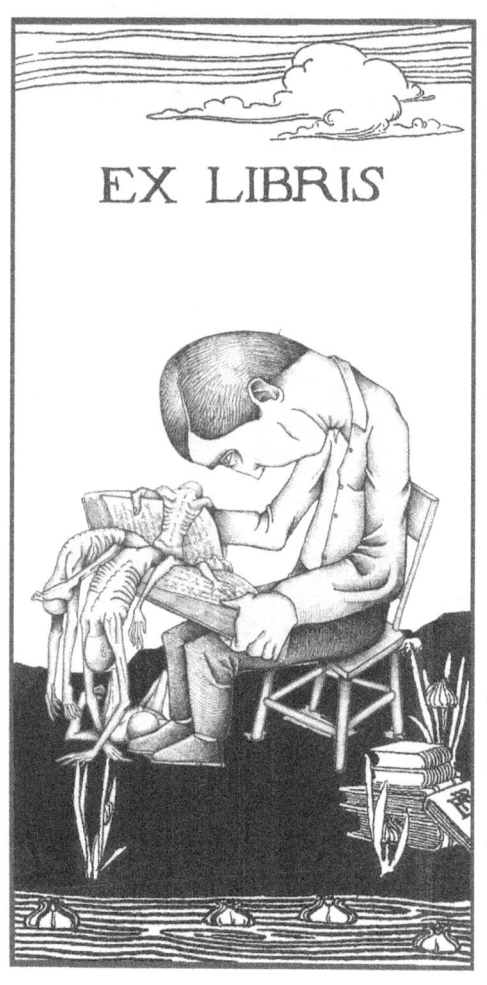

EX LIBRIS

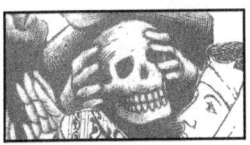

The
WILLIAM SCHAFF
Choosable
Affordable
Wonderful
Gallery
of
ART

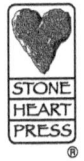

Stone Heart Press • 27 State Street • Warren, RI 02885 U.S.A.
e-mail: stoneheartpress@yahoo.com

Index of Illustrations

*D*edicated to the supporters of

Fort Foreclosure and the arts

that come out of there,

and to my friends in the great town

of Warren, Rhode Island

Opposite:

Bearing History's Burden

1999

10" x 8"

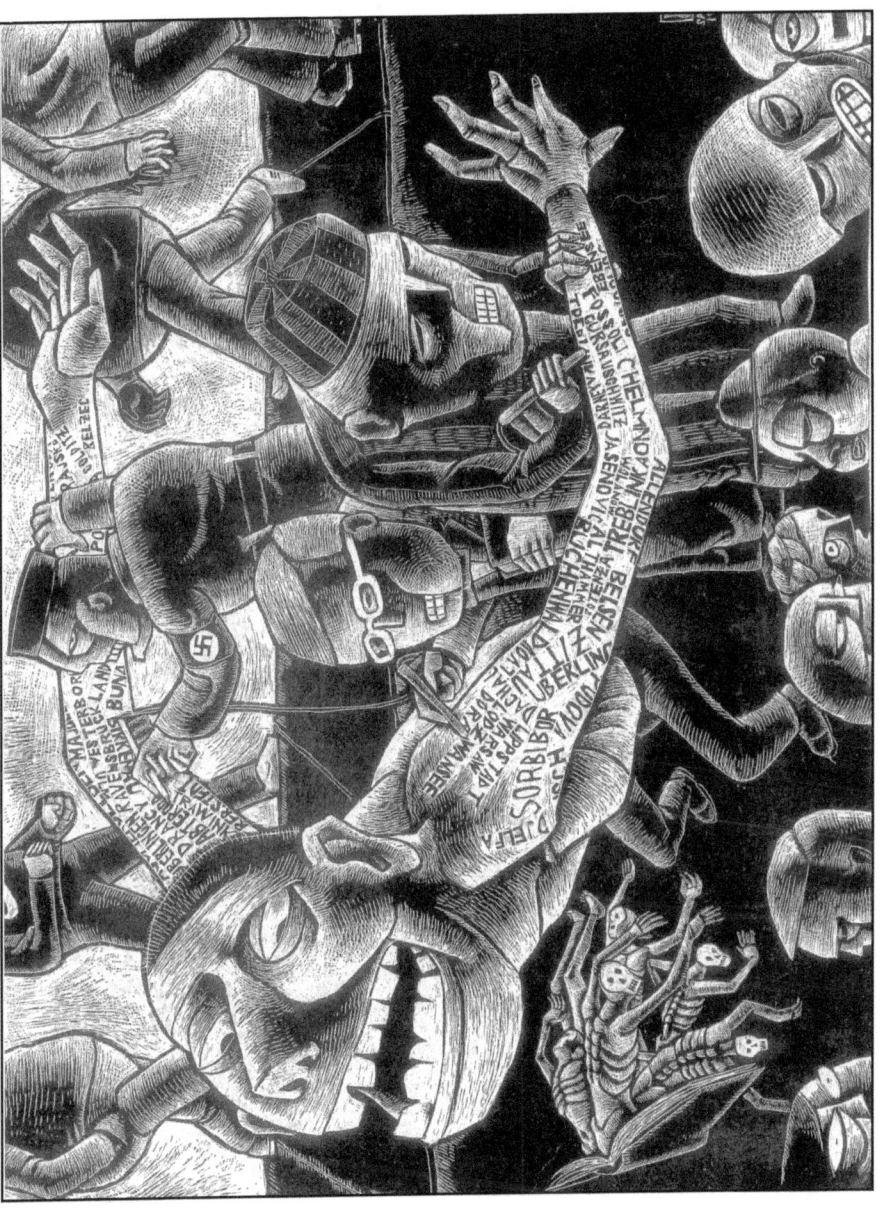

Opposite:

Bilgewater

2015

5" x 7"

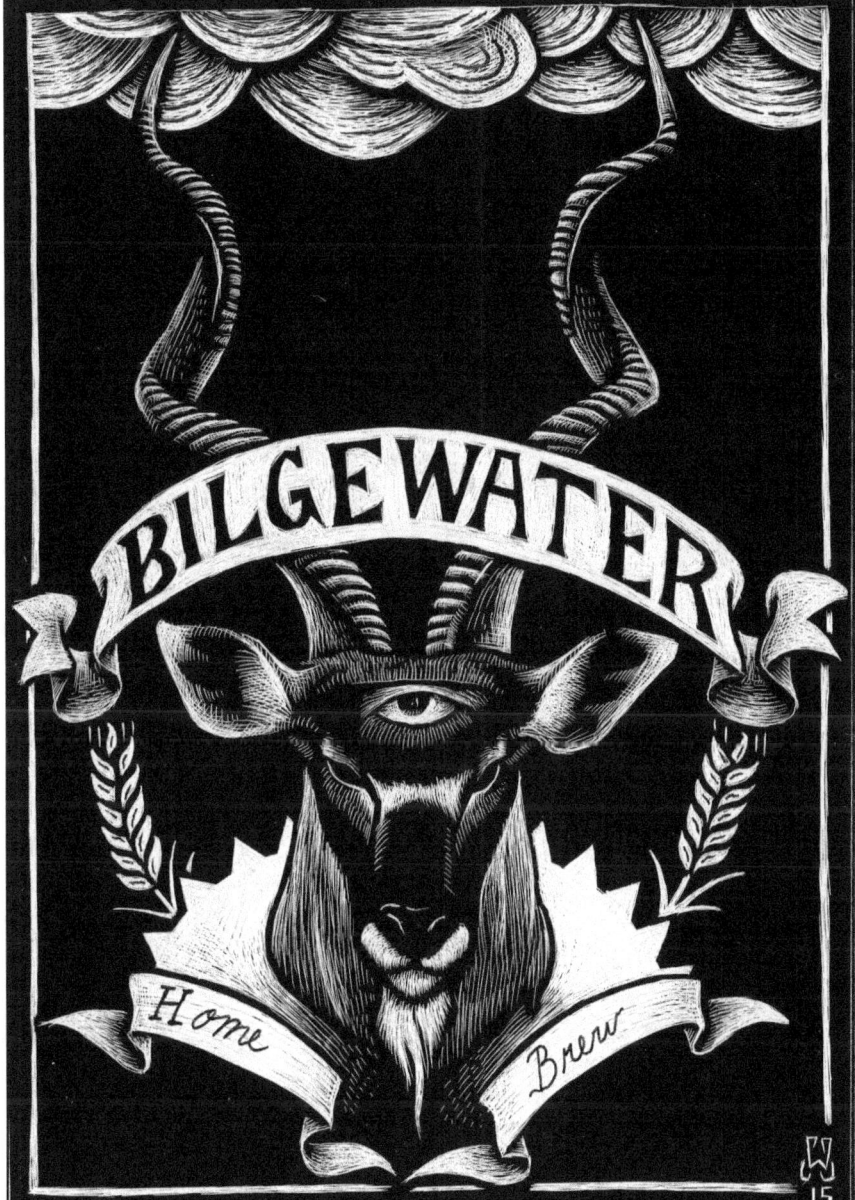

Opposite:

The Black Sheep Dinner Table

2005

10" x 8"

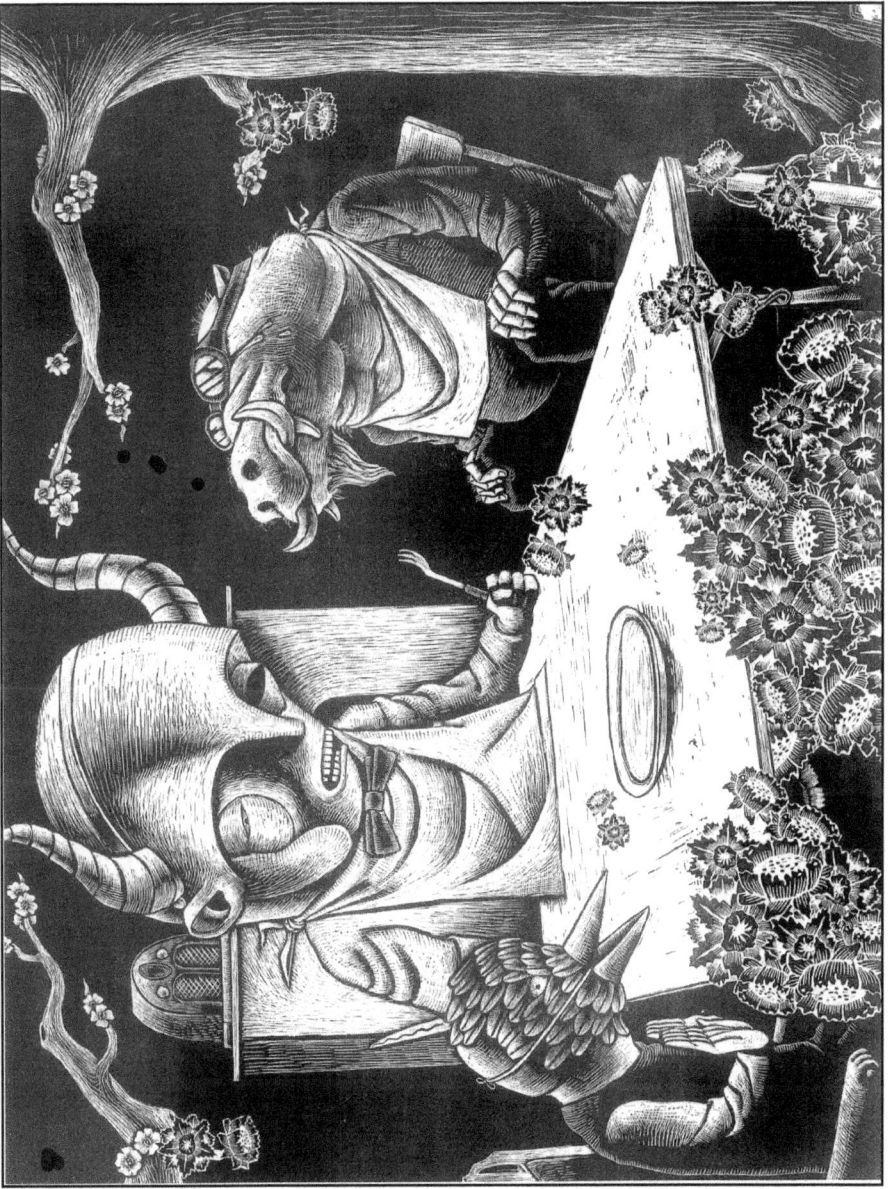

Opposite:

An Octopus for Okkervil River

2005

8" x 12"

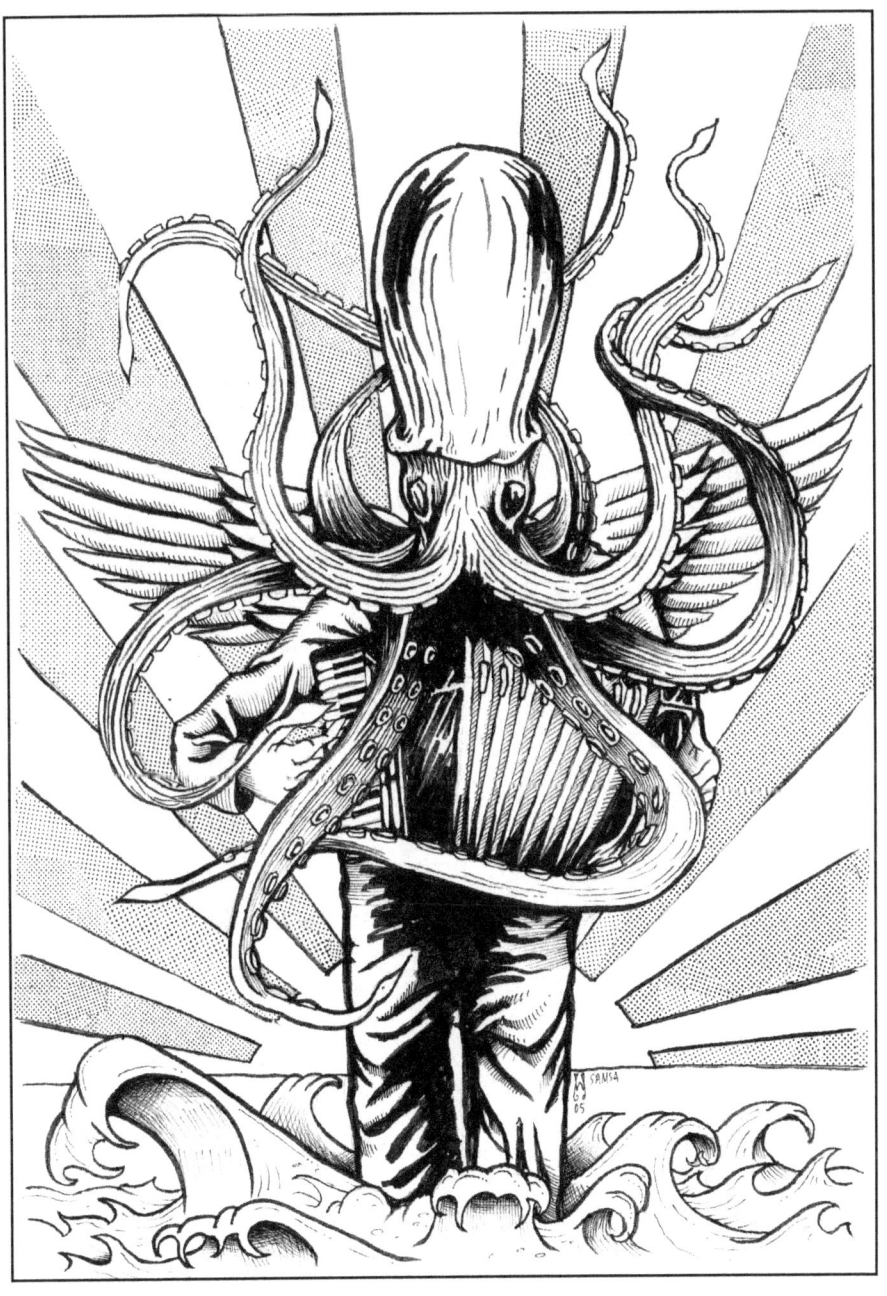

Opposite:

Cancer

2000

7.25" x 11"

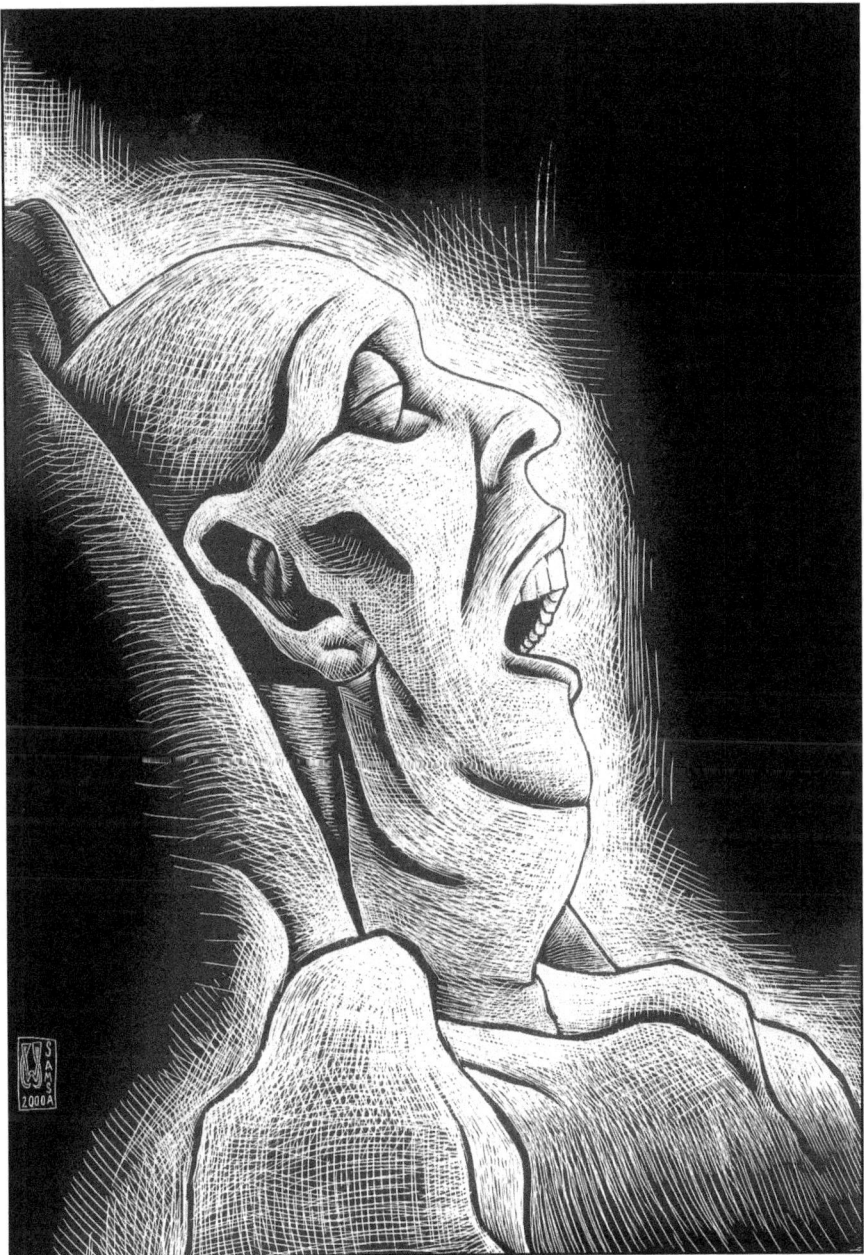

Opposite:

Human Interaction on a New York Train.

2013

16" x 11"

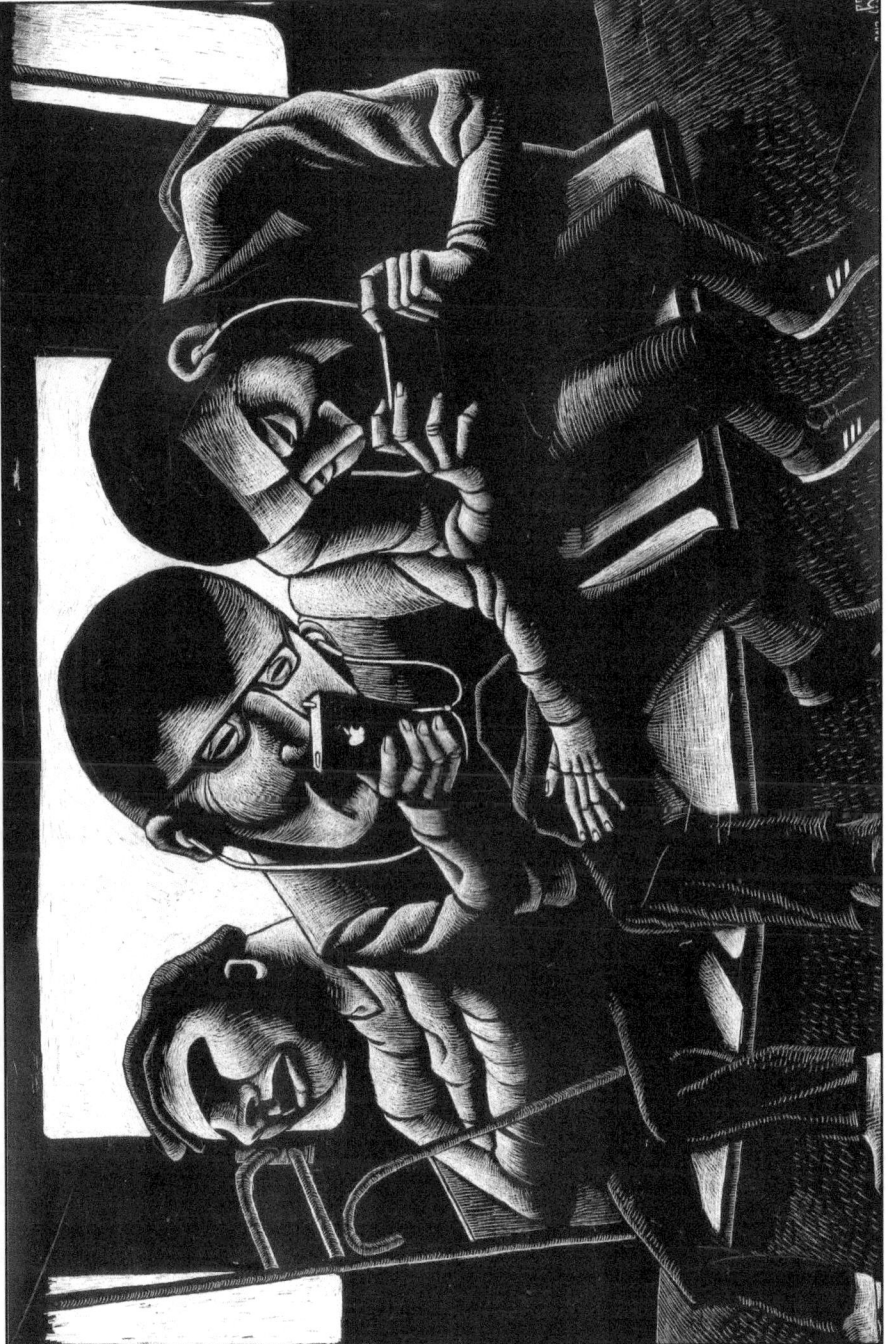

Opposite:

Young Man, Drunk and Asleep

2005

12" x 14"

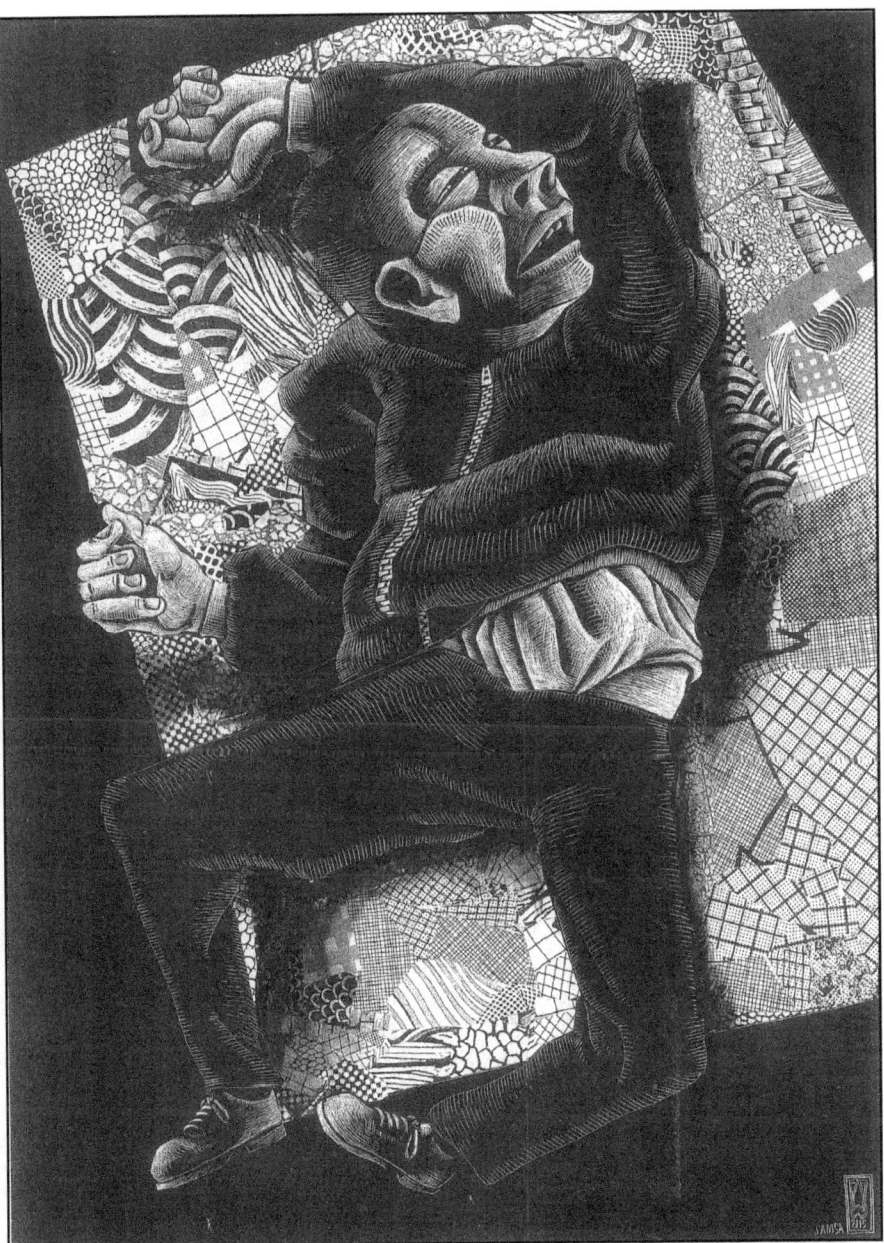

Opposite:

Jesus Washes the Feet of the Disciples

2008

8" x 20"

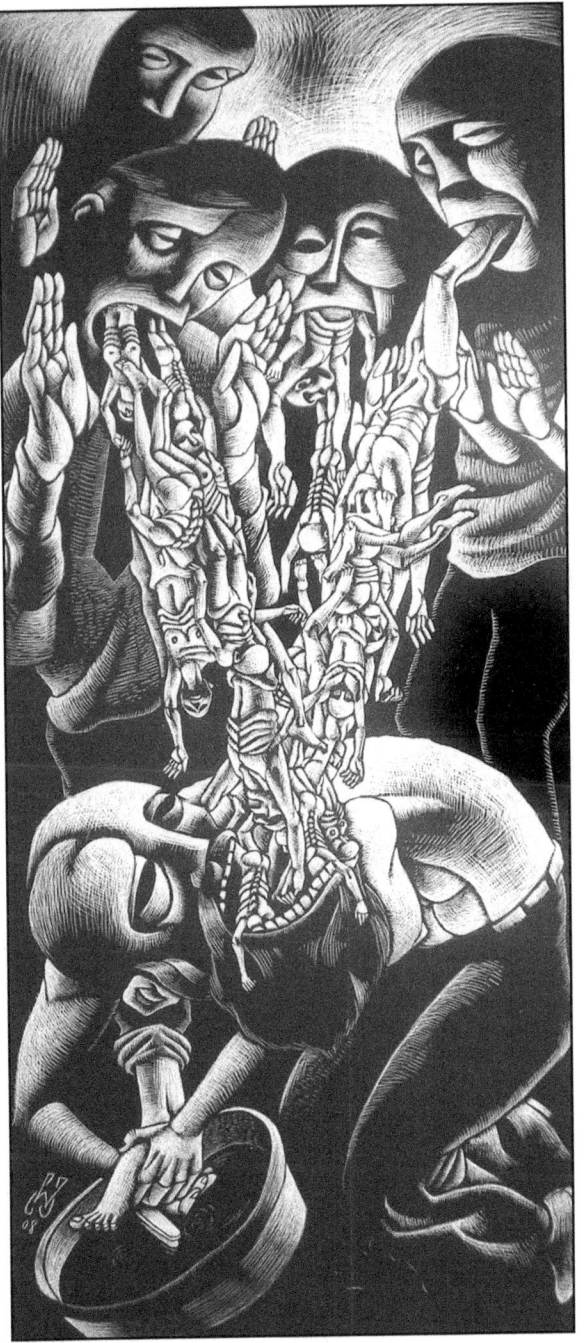

Opposite:

Portrait of a Young Man, Filled With Hate

2008

10" x 13.5"

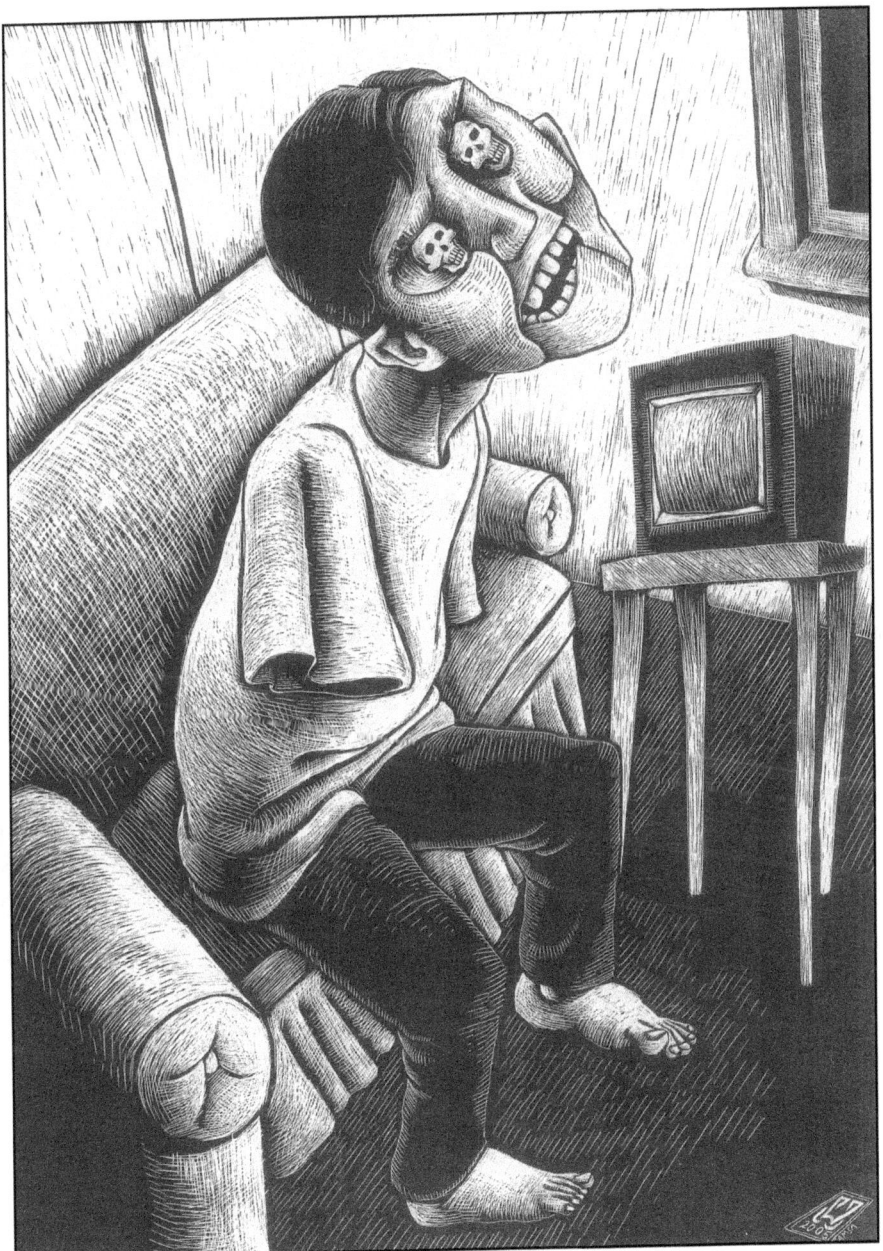

Opposite:

All Thoughts Are Prey to Some Beast

2011

8" x 12"

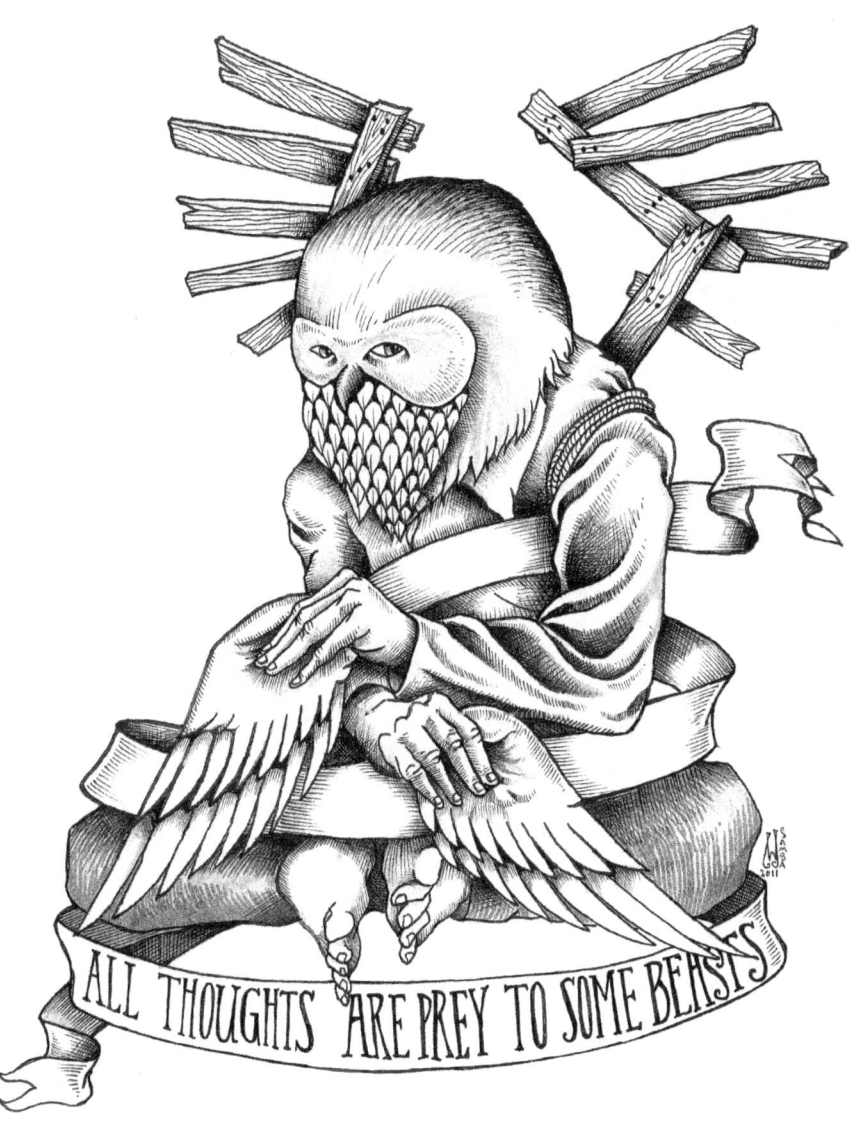

ALL THOUGHTS ARE PREY TO SOME BEASTS

Opposite:

Where Is My Wife?

2002

5.5" x 8.5"

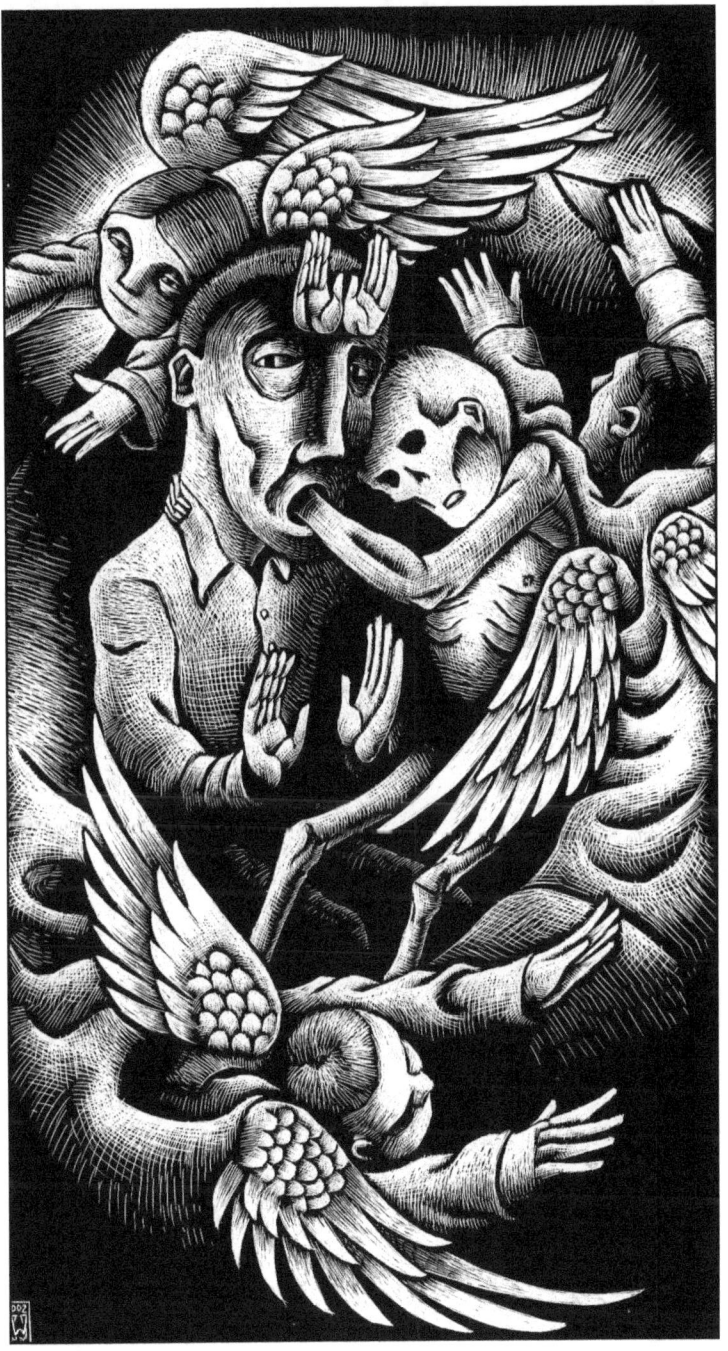

Opposite:

Trying to Remember How It Got So Late

2013

18" x 12.5"

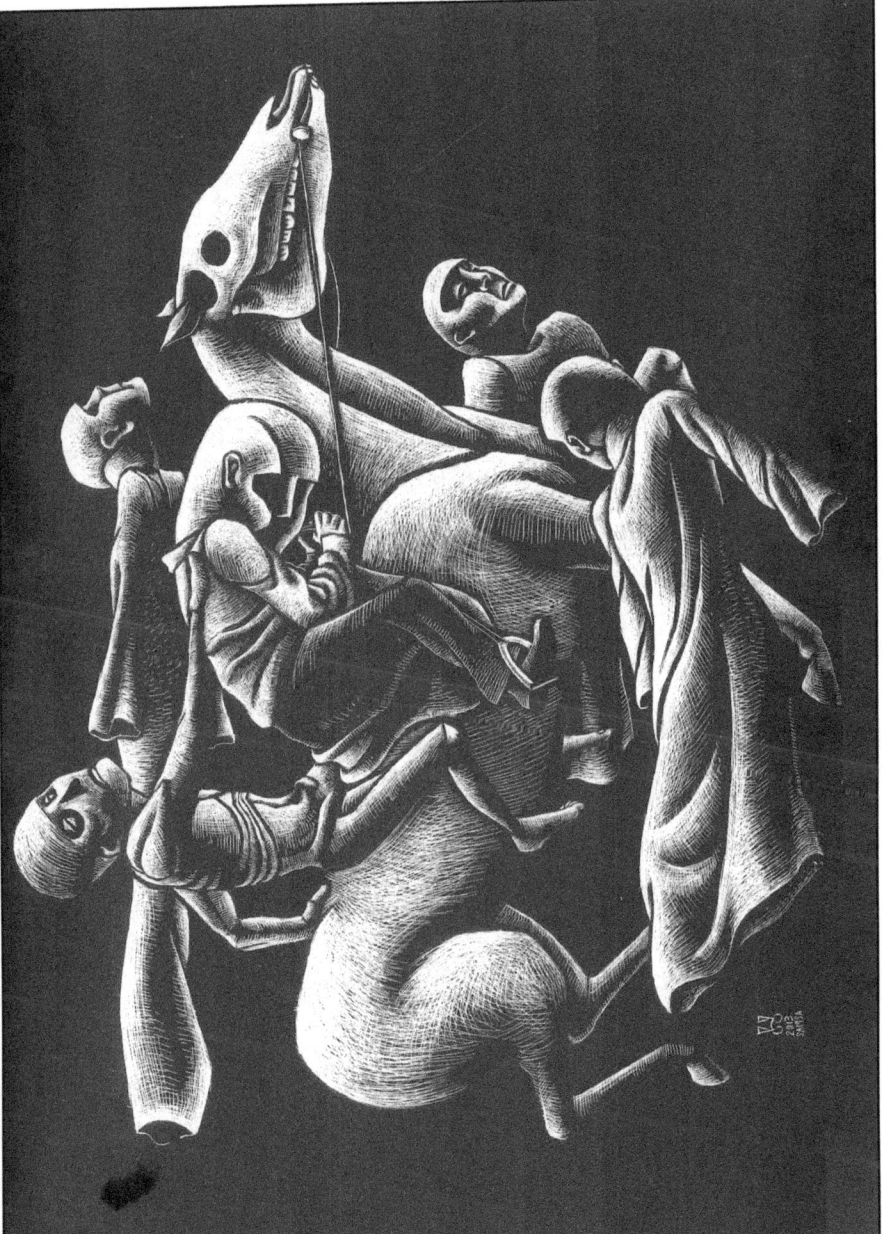

Opposite:

Study of a Sparrow

2001

4.25" x 7.25"

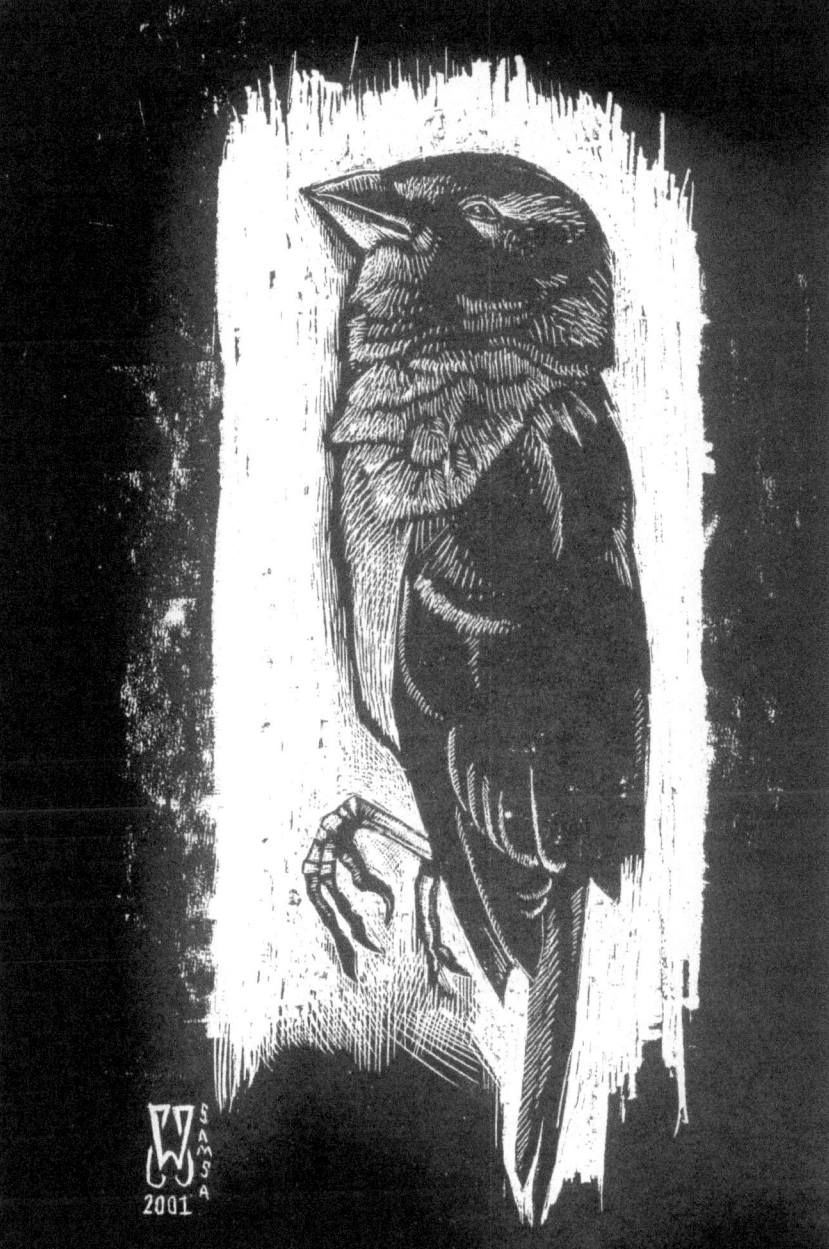

Opposite:

Portrait of a Confused Christian

2003

18" x 24"

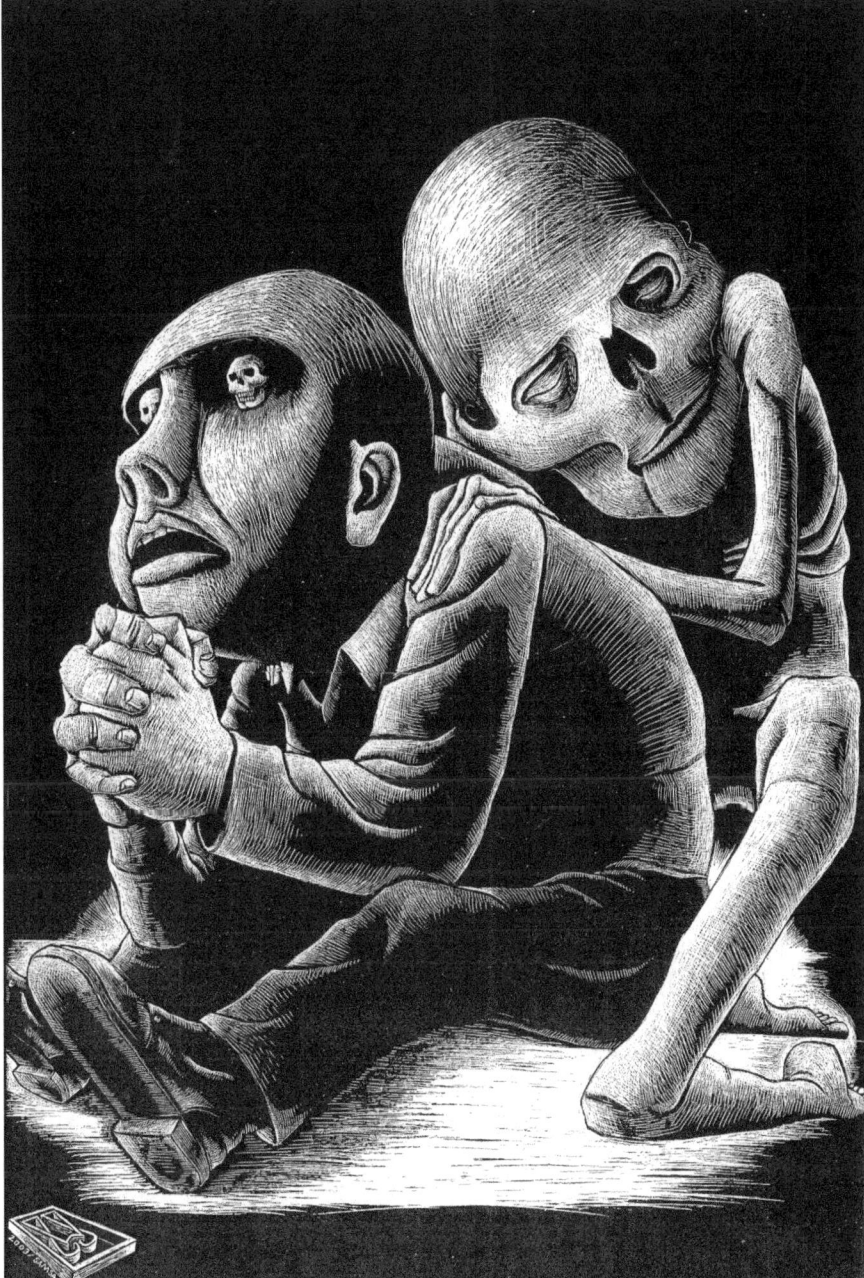

Opposite:

"O Roar of the Universe..."

2012

8" x 12"

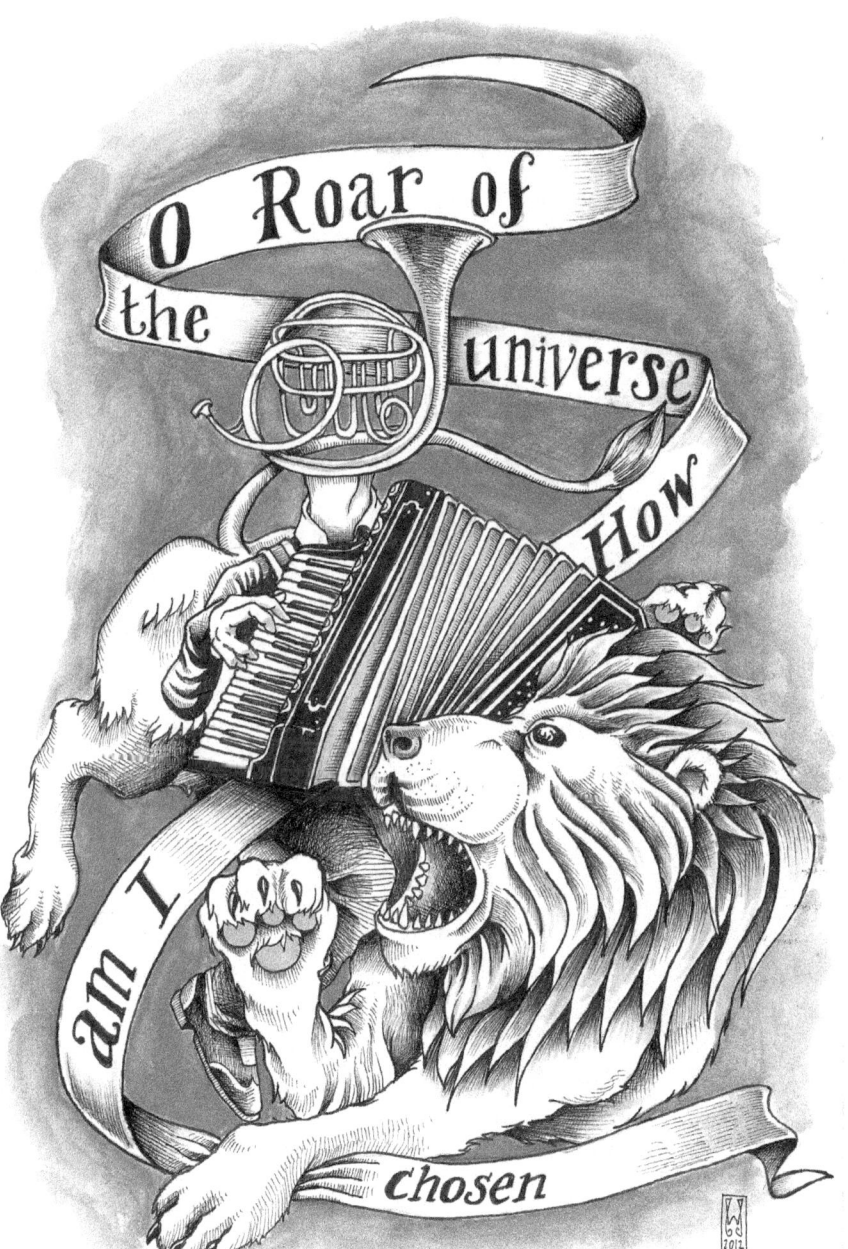

Opposite:

Portrait of Two Men Walking

2007

8.25" x 13"

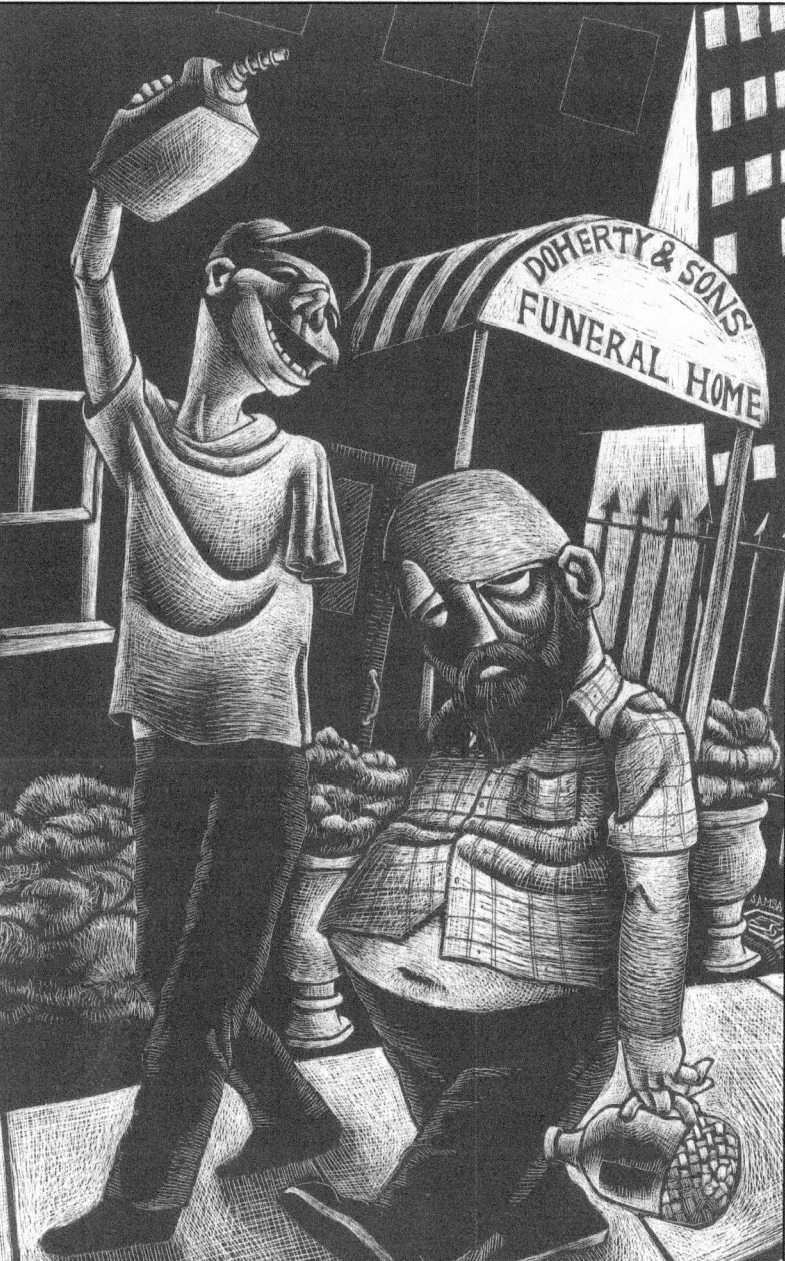

Opposite:

Portrait of a Musselman's Descendant

1999

6.75" x 10"

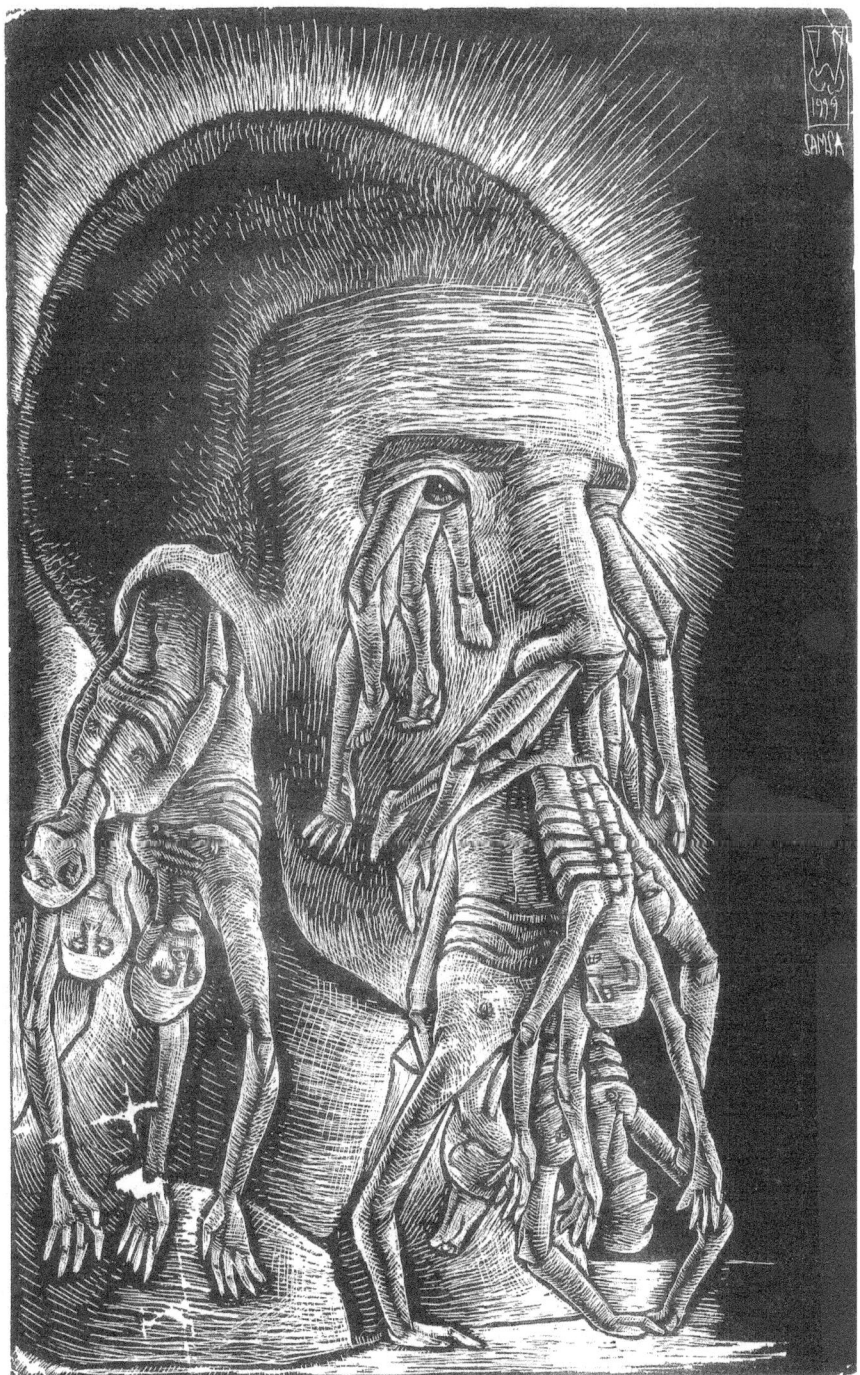

Opposite:

Portrait of a Drunk Boatman

2006

9" x 5.5"

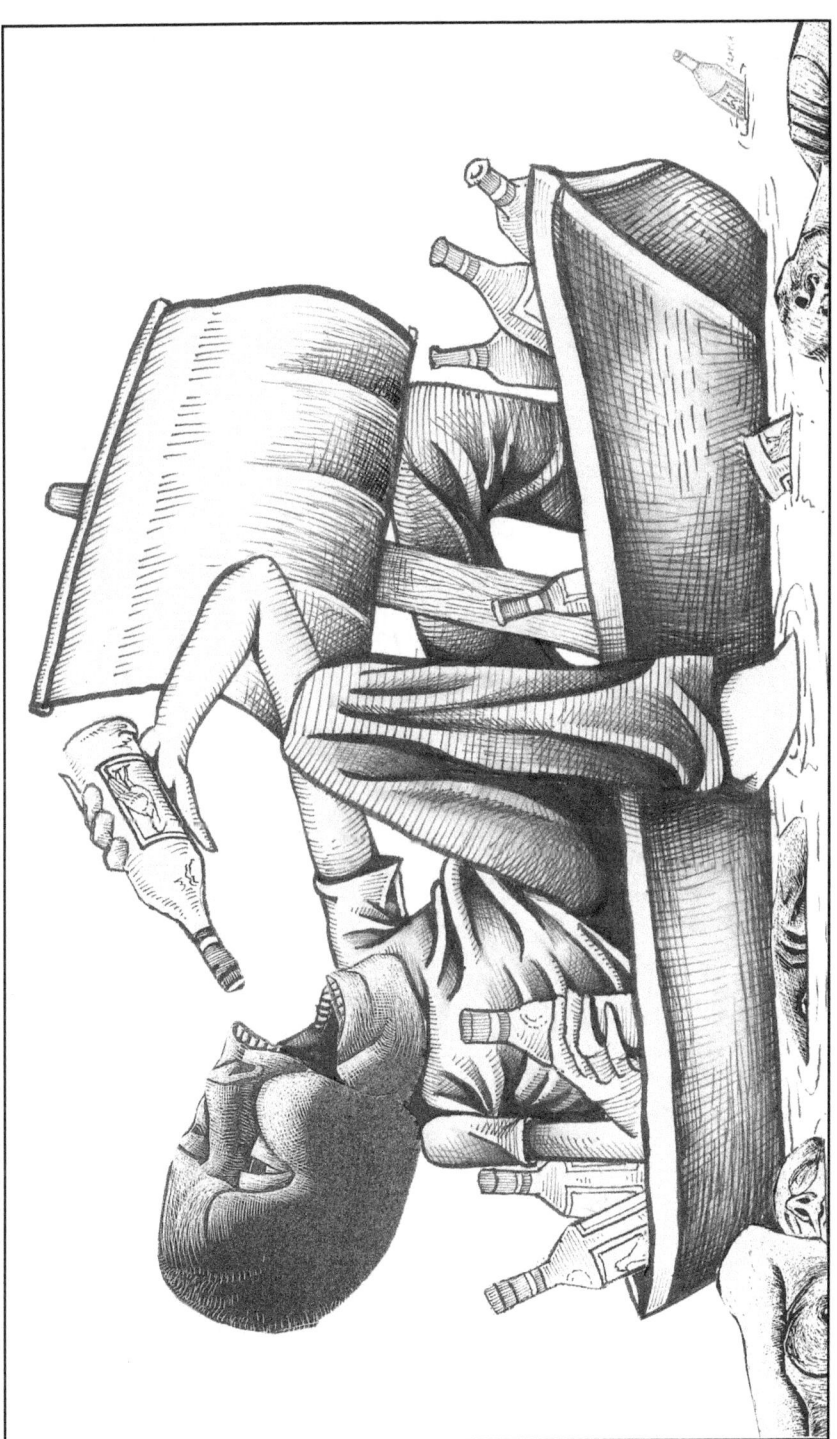

Opposite:

Nowhere to Go

2014

8" x 12"

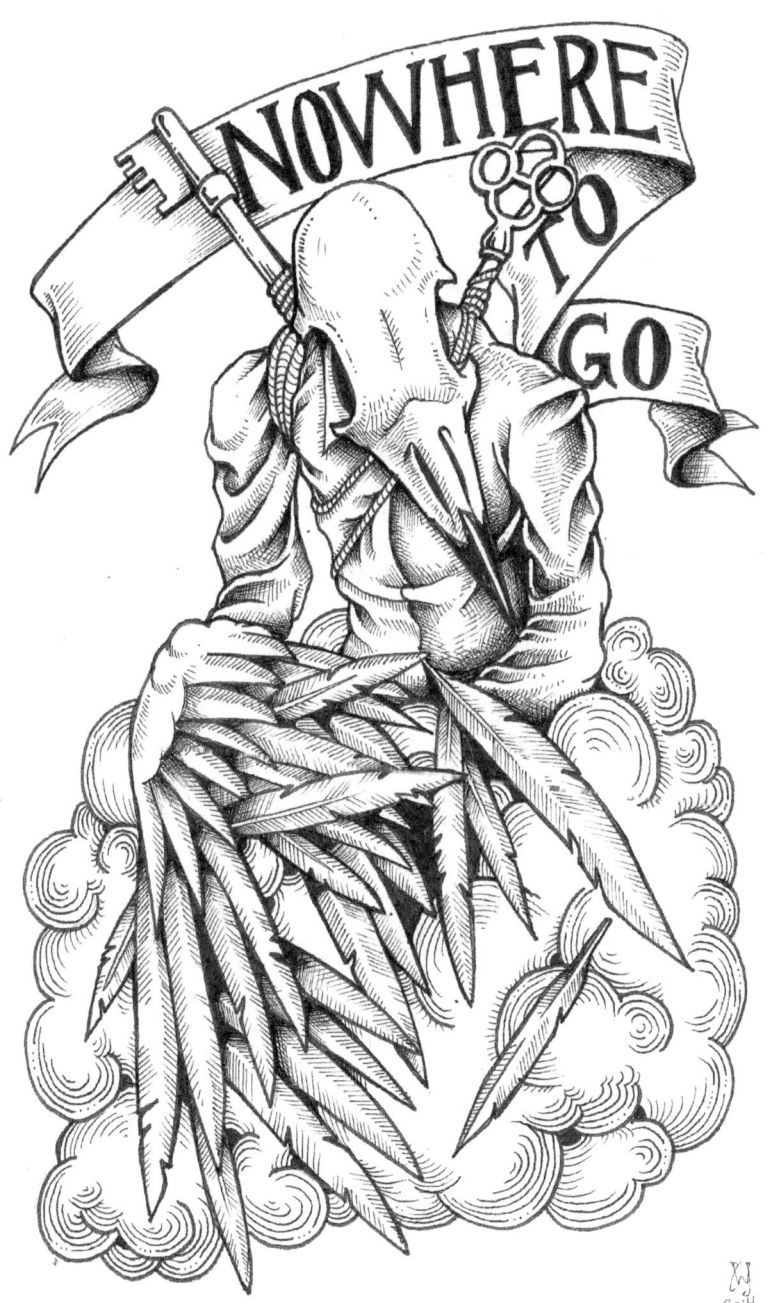

Opposite:

Resilience

2011

6" x 8"

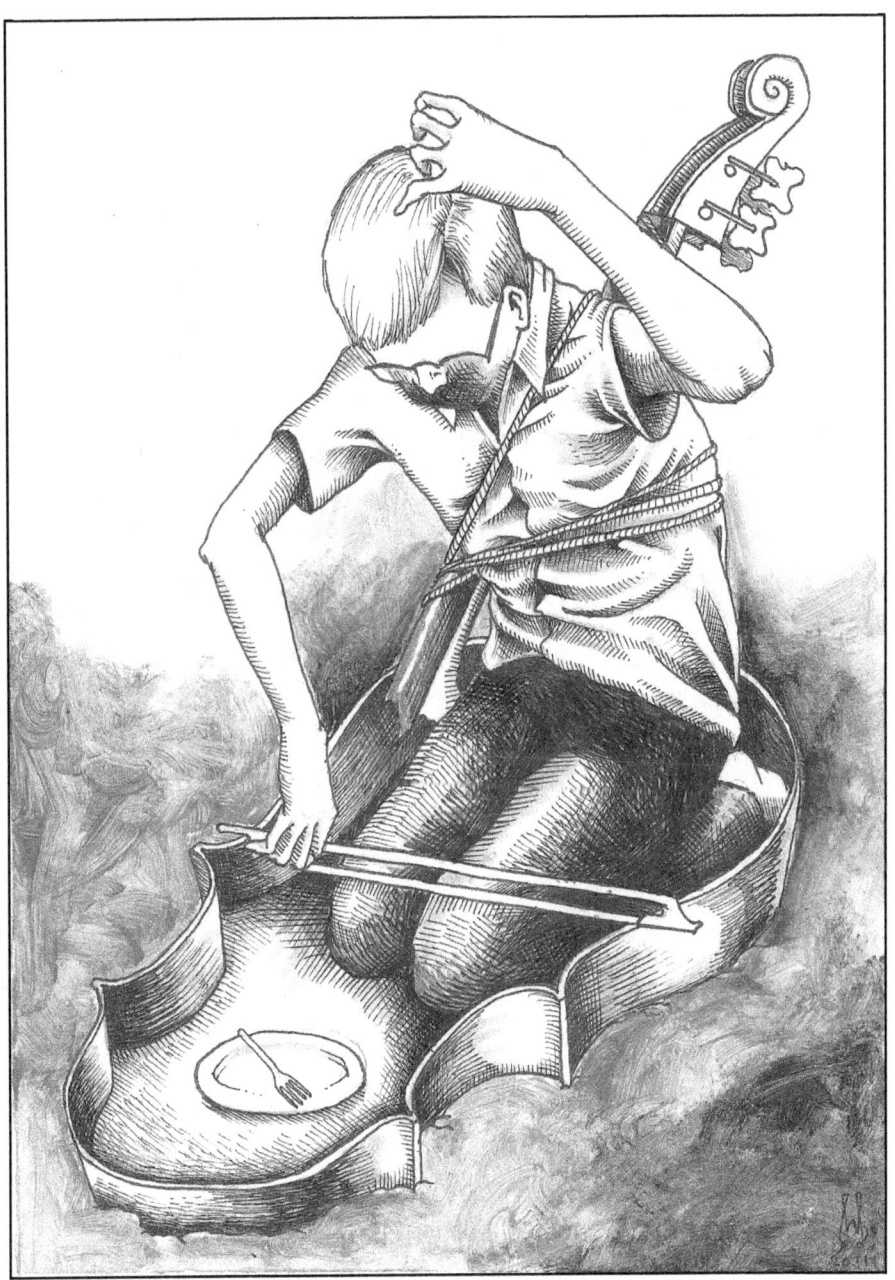

Opposite:

The Titanic, Jr

2006

17" x 11

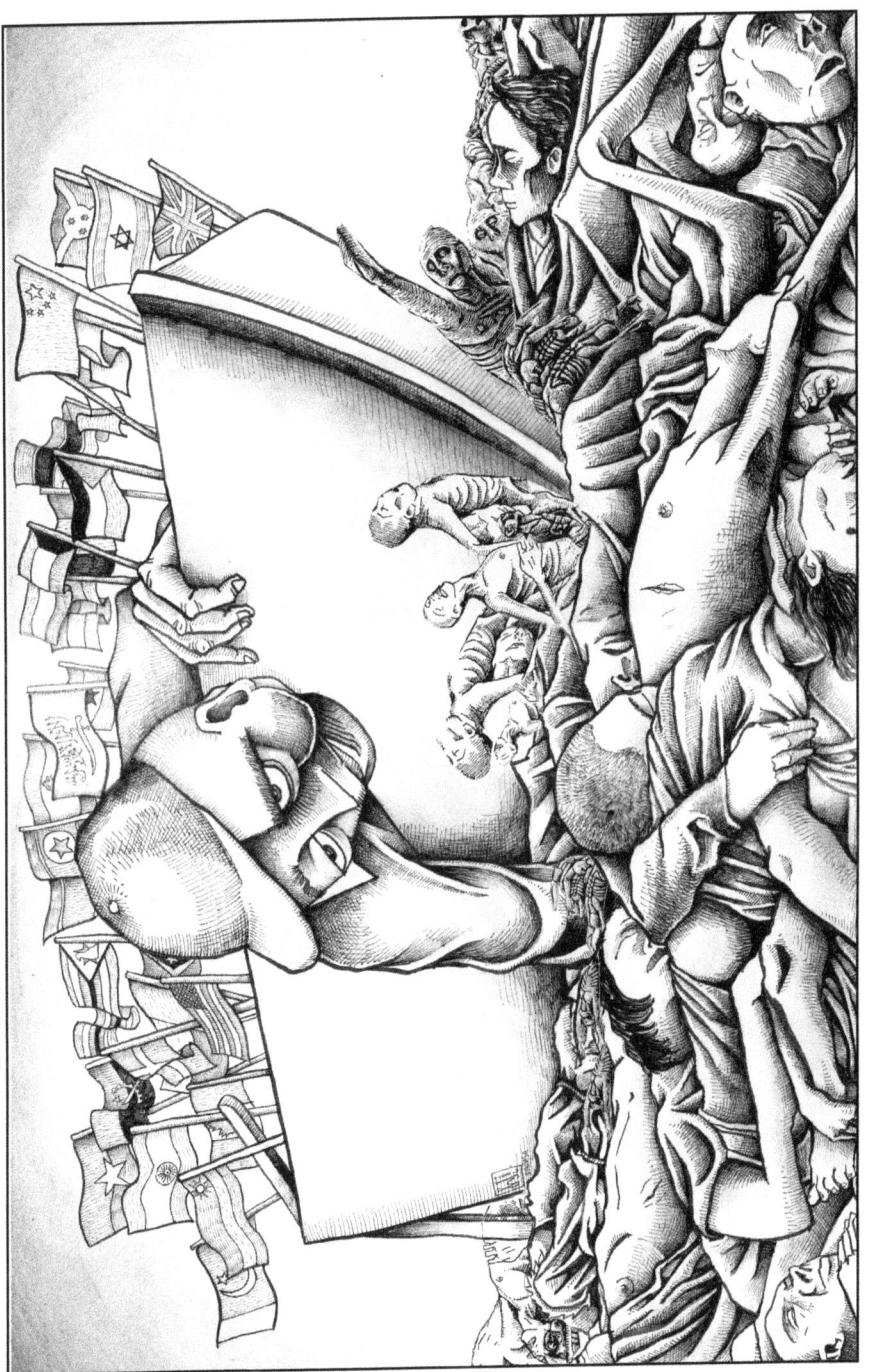

Opposite:

Il Sol

2015

5.5" x 9.5"

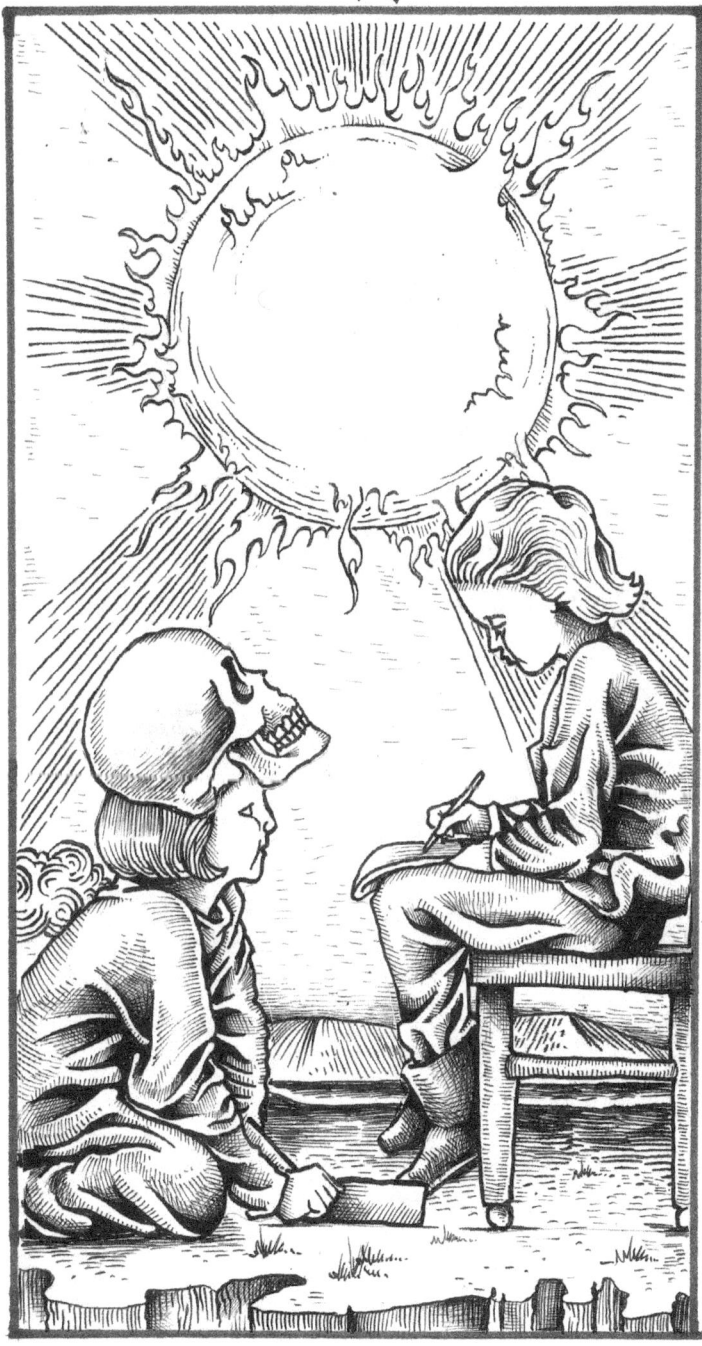

Opposite:

Night Machines

2015

16" x 19"

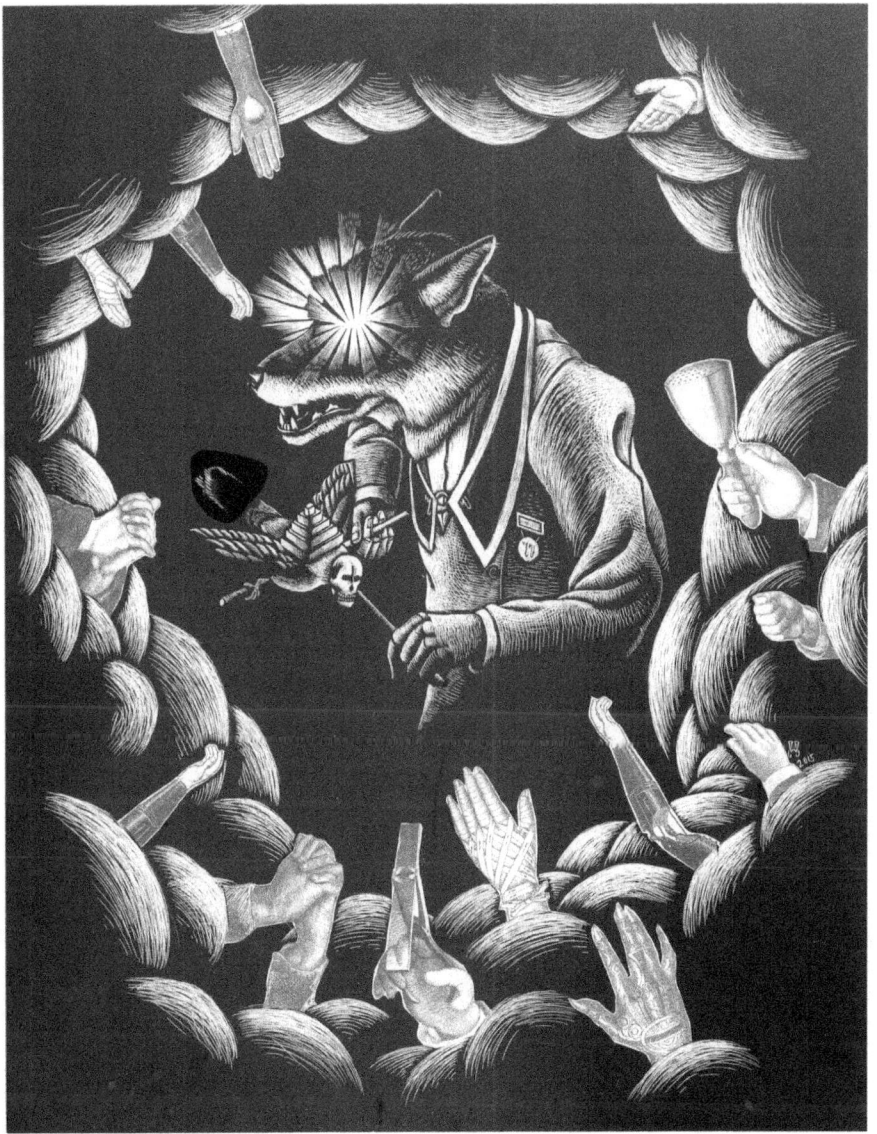

www.ingramcontent.com/pod-product-compliance
Lightning Source LLC
Chambersburg PA
CBHW070337190526
45169CB00005B/1935